KNOW YOUR SELF

STRUGGLE GIVES SUUCEES

R. DHANUSHBHARATH

Made with ♥ on the Notion Press Platform
www.notionpress.com

"NONE CAN DESTROY IRON, BUT ITS OWN RUST CAN! LIKEWISE NONE CAN DESTROY A PERSON, BUT ITS OWN MINDSET CAN!"- RATAN TATA

THE WORLD HAS MOVEING IN ONE

DIRECTION, BUT SOME PEOPLE WANT TO CHANGE THAT. I WANT DEDICATE TO THAT PEOPLE.

"I DON'T THINK LIMITS" - USAIN BOLT

Contents

Contents

About Me

Am a small boy living in the village. My mom and dad work in a private college. Am and my brother studied in the government school. And then the school days are finished. Then joined the Madurai medical college. College life was giving me many struggles and that has been good because that has improved my quality. The struggle has good for everyone's life that made a person a high level and power. And many people go for girls and enjoy. Enjoy giving temporary happiness but you will struggle in your life will soon. So you can improve yourself better than your yesterday level. And don't stand in one place that made you in the same condition and you will expire soon. Be the updated person update only give you the standard one you do not get the update you the old one. The world one improves the updated one only. For example any mobile company and cars then anything updated only living with us. old or un-updated peoples are should leave in the world. And old is having low price and not giving the importance. Any type of medicine and also anything updated only gets the top of importance. And the STRUGGLE GIVE THE UPDATE – UPDATE GIVES THE POWDER- POWER GIVES ANYTHING. Then making the power has not easy that taking

a long time. And the power gives what the next move you do. Taking the power is highly potent. how many people know about THE 48 LOWS OF POWER by ROBERT GREENE? The legends say about the power. The world has moved on by the 48 laws. Most of the powerful people follow the 48 laws. And also we are rolled by this these 48 laws by the powered people. The powered people mostly followed the laws. And am reading the 48 laws of power to give the big vision of power. And it is really interesting and so gives the power. And reading the book gives good knowledge and see the world new vision.

Now how am converted to age 6 than now? So we tell about the power and update to our young generation.

STRUGGLE

UPDATE

POWER

So the struggle is important in your life. the person who handles the battle that makes the perfect person. Who can fear the battle if that person did not come up to the next level in life? So all the plants struggle with born—the starting growth of seed under the earth with the battle. So we can not be disappointed with the battle. All of the world's bio living are having the battle in their life. which can get the correct way to handle the battle that ROLE THE WORLD. The great theory of CHARLES DARWIN through the survival of fittest concept, Where organisms are best adjusted to their environment are the most surviving and reproducing . so by this theory which can update the knowledge are any updated version only can lead the world or only can living in the world. so you can make sure can be updated or not. Then you can be updated you will get the all power or able to live in the world or any work or any this only update can do. The un-updated things are live in the world but did not have any power. Then they are not useful to any person. So finally am give a formula for success (**SUCCESS = STRUGGLE + POWER).** This is the formula for success. Then we see the next my school life.

JOURNEY WITH ORDINARIES

CHAPTER ONE

SCHOOL DAYS

CLASS 1 TO 5

CLASS 1 TO 5 Our life is a good one. We learn about some things in our education but those things are not fully used in our life. Most people have many degrees but they work in an unrelated job that which can they study. School days are the best thing for all people. All of the one day can go to old. That time the school days are college days gives good memory.

I Am in school times am not studying well. The class toppers have created a big image in the class. And those guys are praised by all teachers and principals. And they told me the topers are getting a good job . and having good marks. and having good status in our life.

And then my parents also said to study well get good marks and get a high-level degree and also get Phd that pays you well. They said also educated people have good credibility in our life. So educated people only have all things they said. And then am thinking about the degree. My thought is yes a degree gives good credibility and wealth. So we must get the degree. and then am studying hard for getting the degree. I had one big dream in my school days.

In my school conducting the test every term. The toppers and high-level mark-scored students are going to the school stage and they get the price and all teachers are told about the students. And they said they are good students for our school and they improve our school level. And given the report card, most of the students have high-level marks with a grade of A+. Am not getting high-level marks and an A+ quality. I am just a pass student only. That results are my 2nd standard report. Sometimes I cry because I am not getting good marks and am not able to get a good degree and then life has full damage. Then not having any credibility am lost my life. so am working hard for getting more marks. and one interesting thing is didn't know to write my name in English until my 3rd standard. My mom's sister has told me how to write my name in English.

All my class friends are fun with me has by am didn't know how to write my name in English. And also am writing my name in Tamil not right. My friends read well and write well by am write but fully mistakes. And also read the book in my class full of mistakes. My teachers punished me for not reading the book well.

They tell us to write the same words and lines 100 times. I am having fear of entering the classroom. and the exam days am highly fear because being read well at my home but forgot all things at the time of entering the classroom. When the exam started then am trying to write the exam but that are not right but am writing anything that are having spelling mistakes so learn how to write without spelling mistakes.

CHANGING OF SCHOOL;

One time my family was unable to pay the amount for the education. That time the school principal punished me and my brother. And we have leg pain. That time was am studying 3rd standard. And then my mom and dad asked the principal why did you punish my son. and the principal said I am sorry. my dad said don't do this other students. And then my dad asked me and my brother if we like to change schools. ok dad we move to another school.

And then am and my brother joined the other school. That school has good. the humble teacher and so many new friends. And my new school journey has been so good. And the teachers are giving more importance to my brother and me.

One time the zonal level drawing competition had conducted. That time my brother joined that computation. And my brother gets 1st place in that competition. And my teachers are having big happy for my brother getting that price. And my school has very small then my brother got that price my school is popular in my district. And then my brother qualified at the district level. And that time my brother gets 2nd place in that competition. That gives a big improvement to my school. And many district officers came to my school and give some awards to my brother and my teachers. And also my teacher is invited to our home. then my mom and my brother go to her home. They give some drawing equipment and some awards etc.

Then my brother was famous in my village and in my district. And my brother's photo has come in the newspaper. Then it is a turning point in my school and my family. My brother increased the credibility of my family.

And the days are going on. One day my school introduced the computer. And give some knowledge about the computer. That has special in my school. And I and my friends and all in the computer lab every day. The most interesting thing has that time am studying only 4th standard in my school. Then it is one of the important things in my school journey. And how to paint on the computer and some of the making of the editing and give knowledge about the computer. And then the computer is my world. work a minimum of 2 hours a day. It is a good day in my life and gave the knowledge about computer skills.

And some of the days are gone for the exam have come and my teacher said to study well and write the exam well. That's my 5th standard exam and am writing the exam very well. I get the mark 58 out of 60 marks. That is a good thing in my best examination.

Then one day the computer has not worked. I said to my teacher then she told me to ask my father for help. Am going to speak to my father, because he is knowing about computers. Then my dad comes to my school and he clears the problem with the computer.

And the summer leave has come then we play cricket and many games. We help my father with land work. And my dad gives the money everyday evening for 2ruppes which is the biggest amount at that time. and am and my brother and saving the money for a savings toy.

The summer leave has finished then that school having only upto 5th standard only. Then am going to another school. And leaving the school very sad. My teacher said to study well in your next school.

At that time my brother studying in the school had 3rd standard. he makes the record in that school.

How the record has been made; you make your name in the place for a long time you make the record. That has very big and unable to make any other. And the record gives to you credibility.

" The world only gives respect only for the recorded person so your record is a must in your life. That makes you a very strong person. And that record is your identity. Identity is a must in your life. So make the perfect record and identity. And the record gives the identity. Identity gives the power in your life power gives the success in the vision".

You see the world recorded person only can have an identity in our life. They do the unbelievable thing. For example, CHE GUEVARA makes the most unbelievable thing in history so we all respect Che Guevara. That man is the most power full in history. He does only possible things.

And also "THE BIGGEST POWER IN THE WORLD IS THE VELUPILLAI PRABHAKARAN" am loving the person very much in my life. "My first hero is my dad and then my next hero is my Velupillai prabhakaran". So make the record and that record give to your identity and you're the power full person. The single man turns the world vision to the record.

The most inspiring quote is" IF ONE IS DETERMINED TO DIE FOR THE TRUTH, EVEN A COMMON MAN CAN CREATE HISTORY".

It is my favourite line by the sir. That makes you very confident and makes you such a very powerful. And he is the king of the all-powerful people. Then that man gives inspiration to every youngster. all the people tell his name and producing the power at the time tells about his record and "most important that man's name gives the power to the young people".

So the record only gives the identity and then identity gives the power. You will want the power you make the record. The record gives you identity and then identity gives the **RECORD**

IDENTITY

POWER

So everyone makes the record in their life that not able to beat anyone. Then the power formula is

POWER = RECORD + IDENTITY

SO THAT IS (P = R + I). Then many people have separate records in our life. That record differs for each people. Like usain bolt ,neeraj chopra, sunder pichai and etc. So make your record then the long process and very hard. But you make a record that stands for a long time for you until the record is broken.

Ok, let's see about my next school days.

CLASS 6 TO 10;

Am joined class 6th in a new school. That also the small school and new friends and new teachers.

Joining the new school at that time the headmaster asked them some questions about basic things. That time some tables and spelling headmaster asked. Am said the correct answer.

And that school has good teachers. One teacher has very kind and humble. Most of the students like that teacher. And she tells some discipline and yoga. and the PET teacher is hard work for getting the some the price in a sports events.

At the time of 6th standard, am started to see the circuit matches and going to play cricket games in another village.

Playing cricket gives some happy and physical workout. My best player is virat kohli. He plays the game very style. and go to the gym.

And make a new schedule for my workout. Then am wake up at 5 AM then going go running and gym. That makes my body build up.

THEN next goto class 7th which gives some improvement. the class going on and playing cricket every day. At that time my dream has become a big cricket player. See the cricket match every day and make the body buildup.

One time the school conducted a sports meet. At that time cricket has not allowed but running and other events are allowed.

Am joined in the shotput. 1st place at my school level. Then getting popular at my school level. And make some events am and my friends. Some of the game events and singing competitions etc.

And that time we had the one bull. I favourite that. And every evening is and my brother and my friends are training to the bull that has the best part of the school days.

Am spending a lot of my time with the bull. And that name is singa muthu. And the days are going on. The bull has come very strong. We play every day with him. But my dad doesn't do that it getting angry with you. Then the days are going on. am move to next class.

CLASS WITH UNCLE;

My uncle going to the coaching class for TNPSC. And then am also going to the class. We go to the class every Saturday and Sunday. At that time I am enjoying the journey. the class has so good. And many old age people came to the class. That people are aged 30 to 45 something.

They are run for the getting the marks in the tnpsc exam that marks gives the govt job. Because the government job pays well and is a secure job. My uncle also studies for that. That class has conducted every math test. And give the result.

That day most of the people had sad faces and some people had happy faces. Some people have married and have children. Most people come from a long distance. The travelling expenses are so high. I am thinking about the people. Why they can start any business. that gives them good money then why do they work hard for that?

They study all time but some people only get the job because they waste their money and all thing.

Now am thinking about that **'THEY CAN WASTE THE TIME AND MONEY'. The popular author ROBERT KIYOSAKI** said about people in the **RICH DAD POOR DAD BOOK.**

FAVOURITE" THERE ARE ONLY TWO THINGS YOU CAN INVEST; TIME AND MONEY. OF THE TWO, TIME IS THE MORE IMPORTANT".

This man is the greatest person in my journey and he said many things to inspire me. And the book gives knowledge about money and investing.

And his most important thing has time. He said about TIME is so beautiful in the book. Then not waste your time. Time is the price less one.

When you invest in your time that gives the priceless thing all the legends are investing on the time. And their focus is on how to use the time.

MOST IMPORTANT

TIME

INVEST THE TIME IN THE RIGHT WAY

THAT GIVES ALL THING

And then go to the next class. Now am in class 8. At this time am getting some knowledge about science. Mostly am interested in two subjects one has science and maths. Science is the most beautiful thing in the world that makes all things science. The world has been made by science. Science makes anything and that produces action for all things in the world. My interesting scientist is ISAAC NEWTON.

My favourite quote is ''**MY POWERS ARE ORDINARY. ONLY MY APPLICATION BRINGS ME SUCCESS.**

- Isaac Newton

And study about Newton, That's so interesting and study about newton's law. But these are told before in **''our great scientist THIRUVALLUVAR.**

My favourite law by the newton is 3rd law. FOR EVERY ACTION THERE IS AN EQUAL AND OPPOSITE REACTION.

That is the law for the world's living things. And all the countries are working by this law.

When you think about your future that made you strong and update yourself. So all the popular people are made by the update and those people are making history.

IMPORTANT TIME

All the people are known in their life that time hoe most important, yes that has my ending of the school days. At that time many people had big missing in their lives. And now many people in collage days are working in some company are etc.

And most people do not work in aim in childhood work. Yes, know that am also not studying at my dream college and course.....

But you love the secret that made you strong and gives some way and moves to a happy and good place........

Am believes the secret and knows that it gives the right way to your life.

END OF SCHOOL DAY

AM KNOW ONE THING END OF THE SCHOOL DAY THAT HAS TO BELIEVE THE "SECRET".

CHAPTER TWO

MY DAD CRAVING

MY DAD CRAVING

You know '' the real hero in my life is my dad''. And also know you love your dad. because dad gives the most powerful thing that has ''confident''.

HOW MY DAD INSPIRED ME

My dad has good physical strength and humble person. One day he worked on the land. And heavy rain came but he still work in the rain and he stand very strong. My dad's hand was very strong he lift heavy weights easily.

And I am asking my dad, how are you very strong dad? he said take healthy food and go to the gym then build your body strength. So the most important thing has made your physical strength. So friends make the good physical is must in your life.

At that time my dad age is 45 years old.

Now enter the main topic, in my childhood, my dad told you will become an IAS. Am asks my dad why dad, and he said IAS is the most powerful job.

And you help many people give money and education. My dad tells me most of the time tell ''EDUCATION IS THE

MOST POWERFUL WEAPON IT CAN DO ANYTHING AND EVERYTHING" so you will become a good IAS. It is my dad's craving.

CHAPTER THREE

SOCIETY SAGA

SOCIETY SAGA

We lived in a patterned world. and the world works by many patterns. Then that pattern is produced by some unknown persons.

Ok, then we come to our following lifestyle. You see many people who go to school get a job and work for a long time then get money and die. But they not having any fulfil in their life.

We take one person, first, he going to a school that school teach study well and it gives good mark.

Then that person runs to get a good mark. And study hard to write the 10 mark, 5 mark, 2 mark and etc questions and read for a long time for getting a mark. And reach college then run for percentage. Then the world asks what next?

This is the answer to the 18 years of hard work.

That person gets marks

10th mark – 495/500

12th mark – 590/600

Collagepercentage-98%

Then its results, what next?

That person sees his life back and the school life and that school teaching what? and the college teaching what? It is the result of the following pattern. We following the saga of this society..................

CHAPTER FOUR

TRIGARING AMADELLA

TRIGARING AMADELLA

When you know the truth your brain goes to one of the beautiful worlds.................

The world teaches one secret. That secret tells what is the way to live...............

So first, know yourself then it gives the idea to your aim.................

Love your passion, make a plan to reach that...................

When you go for your aim, it produces very powerful strength .... And that strength gives all things to you...............so love your passion.......................

ENTRY TO THE DEVASTATING WORLD

CHAPTER FIVE

IMPORTANT STAGE OF JOURNEY

IMPORTANT STAGE OF JOURNEY

We all are know , one is the important stage in our life............................

Yes your right it is our teenage life time.................

Ok, why it was very important??????????????????

Am not said it is the very important stage, so many legends are said it is the very important stage in our life..............................

BERNARD ARNAULT,ELON MUSK,JEFF BEZOS,LARRY ELLISON,WARREN BUFFETT,BILL GATES, CARLOS SLIM HELU and etc.......................

These people are said the most important part in your life is teenage..........

Yes it is right, what you have learn and seen in your teenage that has the result in your life..............

So friends make sure that you going to the right way in your teenage part..................

Improve your skill that has the key for your determination.............and invest the time in good one.....................

CHAPTER SIX

SURVIVAL OF FITEST

SURVIVAL OF FITTEST

When you come out from the home or your comfort zone that teaches the big thing ....

That gives the many struggles but you get one of the biggest knowledge that comes to your whole life...........

And you know about the world...............

See many people and them having different types of faces........... you have the struggle to manage these people..........and see many friends ....

The cost of living, when you struggle for food teaches many things because food creates many........

When you don't have money and are unable to buy anything that produces something in your brain.............

So when you live without two things that have ''food and money'' that produce stimulation in your brain................

Ok, just try for one day without food and money ....

That gives one big change in your thought!!!!!!!!!!!!!!!!!!!!!!!!!!!!!!!!!!!!!

CHAPTER SEVEN

THE MAGIC DUST

THE MAGIC DUST

Ok, we come to the next page of the journey it is the turning point in the way and is love this page very much because it gives the keystone to my determination******

Collect the stone and make the fort......because the stones are priceless$$$$$$

That stone are help to build your fort and it produces strong protection for your diamond ....

Am collected the stone and built the fort. And the fort is told to me when you get the diamond am waiting for that diamond........

Because the fort has not fulfilled without the diamond%%%%%%%%

Make one diamond but that diamond is only the best in the world......

That diamond make the demand and that producing the power for you.............

And that diamond gives anything for you............................

CHAPTER EIGHT

MAKE A EMPIRE

MAKE A EMPIRE

All people said, am having a big dream and am going for that and one day it will happen....................

But they don't make any work for that. They said only one-day am will make....................

'One day' they said and they said so many reasons...............

So don't tell any reason for anything make the action next second........ that people only can make empire.............

CHANGING MY SYCOLOGY

CHAPTER NINE

KNOWING THE TRUTH

KNOWING THE TRUTH

When you take the calling in your soul that tells the truth. It said loud and beautiful. then you start speaking to your soul.

Your angel , yes your soul give the way to know the truth.

that truth make the confident to build your empire. But many people didn't know the truth.

SOUL

TRUTH

CONFIDENT

EMPIRE

CHAPTER TEN

SEE THE EVLUTION

SEE THE EVOLUTION

When you know the truth it producing the change in your brain and your work and your knowledge.

Then your work will be see like the legends. That is the evolution in your work that leads to make you strong.

And you see the world very small. It producing one silence in your soul. And your soul will speak to you.

When your soul speak to you not take any advice any one. It is the evolution.

CHAPTER ELEVEN

I RECIVE A CALLING

I RECIVE A CALLING

Your soul make a call for you. When you take the call that tells about your future.

Who speak in the call?

Yes, your soul speak in the call.

When the soul will speak to you?

When you work for your goal the soul will speak with you.

And then connecting the dots......

CHAPTER TWELVE

THE CHAPTER THAT DID NOT TEACH IN YOUR SCHOOL

THE CHAPTER THAT DID NOT TEACH IN YOUR SCHOOL

All the schools teach how to get a mark on the exam. They did not teach any skills or creativity.

They teach only how to work for the company. And the schools treat you like a worker. **THEY TEACH ONLY**

1) How to work for the company?

2) How to write the data?

3) How to improve the company?

4) How to develop the company? They never teach above the book. And they don't have knowledge of the book.

Does my teacher ask the question? And am tell the answer.

And he said, your answer is not in the book.

Then am said see in google, it is a new update you asked question.

He teaches 30years old syllabus. The answer also 30 years old .

But he tells you not read the book. And you will not pass the exam.

What can I do?

So improve your skill and knowledge.

SKY ON IQ

CHAPTER THIRTEEN

KNOWING THE REALITY OF MIDDLE-CLASS AND RICH PEOPLE

KNOWING THE REALITY OF MIDDLE-CLASS AND RICH PEOPLE

Ok, why the rich people can always rich?

Why the poor people can consistently poor?

Do you know the reason?

When you get the answer to this question you will come to the place of rich.

So you must know the solution to this. That made you rich. I know the answer to this, but am did not tell, because when you search you did not forget that and you know many things when you search...................

You search in google now!!!!!!!!!

Super bro you will know the reason.

And you must read this book, "rich dad poor dad" by ROBERT KIYOSAKI...................

That change your thought about rich people and money...............

And it gives the answer for that questions...........

CHAPTER FOURTEEN

PLAN TO MAX

PLAN TO MAX

Your thoughts make your path.

So make a thought always high. Thoughts determine your future and your life style.

Make a plan always high. And work for your own plan and your own goal.

Don't thing the low level. That made the thought low and your goal also the low level.

Your thoughts having more power. So make a good thought and high level thing. ''DREAM BIG''

CHAPTER FIFTEEN

KNOWING THY SELF

KNOWING THYSELF

Knowing thy self is most important for your goal.

It gives a result that has your capacity and your potential level.

Knowing thy self is the difficult one but it is a beautiful one.

And most people did not know that.

"First, know yourself then make a plan to max"

CHAPTER SIXTEEN

UNDERSTAND THE GAME WHERE THEY PLAYED

UNDERSTAND THE GAME WARE THEY PLAYED

Now you connect the all dots it gives result in your brain.

I think you have big change in your thought.

Now start your game.

LOADING.................. START

History

RESULT: YOU WILL MAKE THE HISTORY.

Know

CHANGE: KNOW YOUR SELF

Powerfull People

"IF ONE IS DETERMINED TO DIE FOR TRUTH, EVEN A COMMON MAN CREATE HISTORY". - VELUPILLAI PRABHAKARAN

"LET THE WORLD CHANGE YOU AND YOU CAN CHANGE THE WORLD". - CHE GUEVARA

"YOUR EDUCATION BEGINS WHEN YOU LEAVE SCHOOL. NOT WHEN YOU'RE IN SCHOOL". ROBERT KIYOSAKI

"IF YOU DON'T BELIEVE YOU ARE THE BEST, THEN YOU WILL NEVER ACHIEVE ALL THAT YOU ARE CAPABLE OF". - CRISTIANO RONALDO

"PATIENCE IS A VIRTUE, AND I'M LEARNING PATIENCE. IT'S A TOUGH LESSON". - ELON MUSK

"THE ONLY WAY TO DO GREAT WORK IS TO LOVE WHAT YOU DO". - STEVE JOBS

"IF YOU DON'T FIND A WAY TO MAKE MONEY WHILE YOU SLEEP, YOU WILL WORK UNTIL YOU DIE". -WARREN BUFFETT

YES MY FATHER IS NOT A RICH PERSON, BUT VERY SOON HE WILL GOING TO BE THE FATHER OF RICHEST PERSON$

Contact

PHONE: 9489024914 EMAIL: dhanushbharath517@gmail.com

Go

WILL SOON

Printed by Libri Plureos GmbH in Hamburg, Germany